Fast Facts About Bugs & Spiders

Fast Facts About
GRASSHOPPERS

by Julia Garstecki

PEBBLE
a capstone imprint

Pebble Emerge is published by Pebble, an imprint of Capstone.
1710 Roe Crest Drive, North Mankato, Minnesota 56003
www.capstonepub.com

Copyright © 2021 by Capstone. All rights reserved. No part of this publication may be reproduced in whole or in part, or stored in a retrieval system, or transmitted in any form or by any means, electronic, mechanical, photocopying, recording, or otherwise, without written permission of the publisher.

Library of Congress Cataloging-in-Publication Data
Names: Garstecki, Julia, author.
Title: Fast facts about grasshoppers / by Julia Garstecki.
Description: North Mankato, MN : Pebble, an imprint of Capstone, [2021] | Series: Fast facts about bugs & spiders | Includes bibliographical references and index. | Audience: Ages 6–8 | Audience: Grades 2–3 | Summary: "What's that jumping by? Meet the grasshopper! Young readers will get the fast facts on these long-legged insects as they learn about grasshopper body parts, habitats, and life cycles. Along the way, they will also uncover surprising and fascinating facts! Simple text, close-up photos, and a fun activity make this a perfect introduction to the hopping world of grasshoppers." —Provided by publisher.
Identifiers: LCCN 2020031928 (print) | LCCN 2020031929 (ebook) | ISBN 9781977131522 (hardcover) | ISBN 9781977132697 (paperback) | ISBN 9781977154200 (pdf) | ISBN 9781977155917 (kindle edition)
Subjects: LCSH: Grasshoppers—Juvenile literature.
Classification: LCC QL508.A2 G287 2021 (print) | LCC QL508.A2 (ebook) | DDC 595.7/26—dc23
LC record available at https://lccn.loc.gov/2020031928
LC ebook record available at https://lccn.loc.gov/2020031929

Image Credits
Dreamstime: Pzromashka, 9; Science Source: Stephen Dalton, 15; Shutterstock: Aottorio, 17, CapturePB, 20 (middle), Daniel Andis, 19, Eric Isselee, cover, Jen Watson, 11, Martin Mecnarowski, 12, Matt Jeppson, 5, Paul Reeves Photography, 13, riphoto3, 20 (bottom left), Silvia Dubois, 4, Somyot Mali-ngam, 8, Thanakorn Hongphan, 18, Vasilius, 20 (top), Vita Zaparovana, 7, Vladimir VK, 20 (bottom right), zabavina (background), cover and throughout; Svetlana Zhurkin, 21

Editorial Credits
Editor: Abby Huff; Designer: Hilary Wacholz; Media Researcher: Jo Miller; Production Specialist: Tori Abraham

All internet sites appearing in back matter were available and accurate when this book was sent to press.

Table of Contents

All About Grasshoppers 4

Eat, Eat, Eat 8

Staying Safe 12

A Grasshopper's Life 16

Fun Facts 18

    Make a Grasshopper 20

    Glossary 22

    Read More 23

    Internet Sites 23

    Index 24

Words in **bold** are in the glossary.

All About Grasshoppers

Hop! What is jumping in the grass? It's a grasshopper! It is an **insect**. Grasshoppers live around the world. But not where it is very cold all year long.

There are about 11,000 kinds of grasshoppers. Many are green or brown. Some are colorful. The biggest are longer than a clothespin. The smallest fit on a dime.

A grasshopper has three body sections. It has two large eyes on its head. They see all around. It also has two **antennae**. These smell and feel.

Grasshoppers walk on six legs. The back two are long and strong. They are great for jumping. Most grasshoppers have two pairs of wings. They can fly through the air.

Eat, Eat, Eat

Grasshoppers eat plants. Some feed on many kinds of plants. Others eat only one. They mostly munch on leaves. But they may also eat stems, flowers, and seeds.

mouthparts

Grasshoppers have chewing mouthparts. These parts cut food like scissors. They move from side to side.

Some grasshoppers cause problems for people. They are **pests**. They eat too many plants. This hurts gardens. It also hurts crops grown by farmers.

Sometimes many grasshoppers come together. This is called a **swarm**. They eat all the plants in one place. They fly to a new spot and eat again. It's a big problem.

a swarm in Kenya

Staying Safe

Grasshoppers need to watch out. They have many **predators**. Animals want to eat them! Birds, spiders, and snakes are just a few.

Grasshoppers will hide. The color of their bodies helps. Green grasshoppers hide in grass or plants. Brown ones stay near the ground. They blend in with dirt or sand.

Grasshoppers have other tricks to stay safe. Some make stinky smells. Others spit brown goo. They do this to scare off predators.

Grasshoppers will also try to get away from danger. Ones with wings will fly. Almost all grasshoppers will use their legs. They kick. Then they jump away.

A Grasshopper's Life

A female grasshopper lays eggs in the dirt. Each egg hatches a young insect. It is called a **nymph**. It looks like a tiny grasshopper. It does not have wings yet.

The nymph eats and gets bigger. It sheds its skin, or **molts**, as it grows. Finally, it grows wings. It is an adult. Jump! Goodbye!

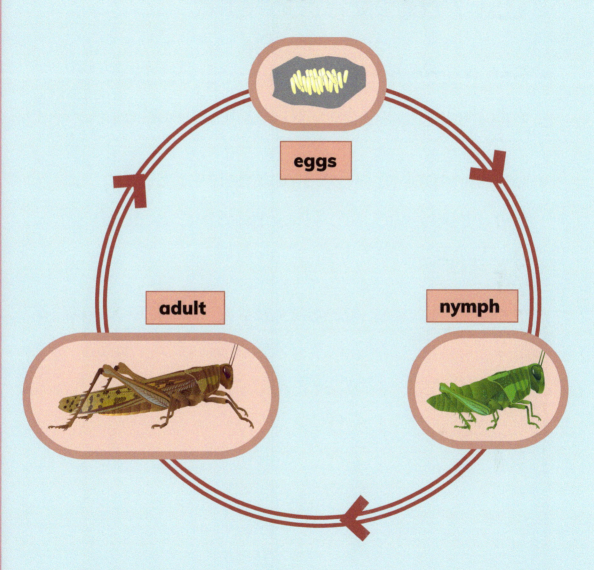

Fun Facts

- Some grasshoppers make sounds! They rub their back legs against their bodies.

- Grasshoppers have small holes on their third body section. They breathe through the holes.

breathing holes

fried grasshoppers

- In some places, people eat grasshoppers. The insects are high in protein. People need protein to be healthy.

- A grasshopper can jump 20 times its body length. If a person jumped like that, he or she could hop over three school buses!

Make a Grasshopper

What You Need:

- clothespin
- green and black markers
- two green pipe cleaners
- scissors

What You Do:

1. Color the clothespin green. Draw two eyes with the black marker.

2. Pull one pipe cleaner through the metal circle on the clothespin. Bend the pipe cleaner to make the long back legs.

3. Cut the second pipe cleaner in half. Clamp both pieces in the clothespin. Bend them to make the front legs.

Glossary

antenna (an-TEH-nuh)—a feeler on an insect's head used to touch and smell

insect (IN-sekt)—a small animal with a hard outer shell, six legs, three body sections, and two antennae

molt (MOLT)—to shed an outer layer of skin; after molting, a new covering grows

nymph (NIMF)—a young form of an insect; nymphs grow into adults by molting many times

pest (PEST)—an animal that is bothersome or harmful to humans

predator (PRED-uh-tur)—an animal that hunts other animals for food

swarm (SWARM)—a large group of animals moving or flying together

Read More

Morlock, Rachael. *Grasshoppers Up Close.* New York: PowerKids Press, 2020.

Murray, Julie. *Grasshoppers.* Minneapolis: Abdo Publishing, 2020.

Peterson, Megan Cooley. *Grand Grasshoppers: A 4D Book.* North Mankato, MN: Pebble, 2019.

Internet Sites

Bug Facts: Grasshopper
bugfacts.net/grasshopper.php

DK Find Out!: Grasshoppers and Crickets
dkfindout.com/us/animals-and-nature/insects/grasshoppers-and-crickets/

Ducksters: Grasshopper
ducksters.com/animals/grasshopper.php

Index

bodies, 6, 9, 13, 18

colors, 5, 13

dirt, 13, 16

eating, 8–9, 10, 19
eggs, 16

food, 8, 9

habitats, 4
hiding, 13

insects, 4

jumping, 4, 6, 14, 19

kinds, 5

life cycles, 16

molting, 16

nymphs, 16

pests, 10
plants, 8, 10
predators, 12, 14

sizes, 5
spitting, 14
swarms, 10

wings, 6, 14, 16